BASEBALL TRIVIA AND FUN BOOK

by Bruce Weber

Illustrated by Lillian Lovitt

SCHOLASTIC INC.
New York   Toronto   London   Auckland   Sydney

No part of this publication may be reproduced in whole or in part, or stored in a retrieval system, or transmitted in any form or by any means, electronic, mechanical, photocopying, recording, or otherwise, without written permission of the publisher. For information regarding permission, write to Scholastic Inc., 730 Broadway, New York, NY 10003.

ISBN 0-590-47174-0

12 11 10 9 8 7 6 5 4 3 2 1   3 4 5 6 7 8/9

Printed in the U.S.A.   40

First Scholastic printing, May 1993

INTRODUCTION

Sports writers love to call sports the world of fun and games. And baseball, the national pastime, leads the way. Throughout its long history, baseball has had its share of great moments — and its share of wacky moments. You'll find the best of both worlds right here in the *Baseball Trivia and Fun Book*.

Use your knowledge of the game and your quiz- and puzzle-solving skills to get the inside scoop. You'll have fun and learn things about baseball that you never knew. Chances are, you'll know some of the answers!

So grab your pencil and step up to the plate. Now, here comes the pitch. Hurry! Turn the page! Enjoy!

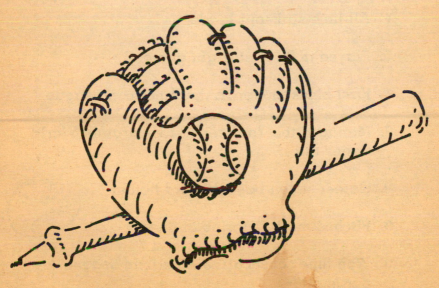

STARTING LINEUP

Match up the clues in Column I with the answers in Column II. Then write the letters in the blanks at the bottom of the opposite page.

I

1. All-time home-run leader

2. Last batter to hit .400

3. A's slugger traded to Texas

4. All-time strikeout leader

5. Played in 2,130 straight games

6. First black player in the American League

7. Managed the Yankees to five straight World Series titles

8. Career stolen-bases record holder

9. Pitched most victories in history

10. Won nine consecutive American League batting titles

II

A. Lou Gehrig

B. Jose Canseco

C. Ty Cobb

D. Rickey Henderson

E. Casey Stengel

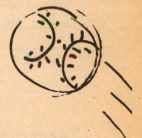

F. Hank Aaron

G. Cy Young

H. Ted Williams

I. Larry Doby

J. Nolan Ryan

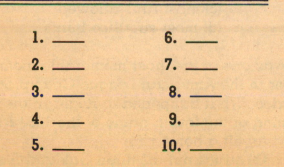

1. ___   6. ___

2. ___   7. ___

3. ___   8. ___

4. ___   9. ___

5. ___   10. ___

COVER QUIZ #1

Roger Clemens

So you think you know everything there is to know about Roger Clemens. Perhaps you do. Try this special multiple choice quiz about one of our star players. Circle the correct answer.

1. Roger was the winning pitcher in the final game of the 1983 College World Series. Which team did he lead to the NCAA Championship?
   - **(a)** University of Texas
   - **(b)** Southern California
   - **(c)** Arizona State
   - **(d)** College of Hard Knocks

2. Among all-time Red Sox pitchers, only Jim Lonborg, Cy Young, Tex Hughson, and Clemens have led the league in an important category. What is it?
   - **(a)** most victories
   - **(b)** most strikeouts
   - **(c)** most runs allowed
   - **(d)** most sacrifice bunts

3. It was one of the most memorable moments ever in the American League Championship Series. What happened to Roger in the second inning of the fourth game of the 1990 ALCS?
   - **(a)** hit a home run
   - **(b)** struck out all three Oakland A's
   - **(c)** walked four straight batters
   - **(d)** was thrown out of the game

4. What's Roger's famous nickname?
        (a) Clem
        (b) Rocket
        (c) The Rabbit
        (d) Jet Man

5. What do super pitchers Roger Clemens, Sandy Koufax, Jim Palmer, and Denny McLain have in common?
    (a) are in Hall of Fame
    (b) won 30 games in a season
    (c) have wives named Stephanie
    (d) won back-to-back Cy Young Awards

6. How long was Roger out of college when he won his first major league game?
        (a) one week
        (b) 11 months
        (c) two years
        (d) three years

7. Roger set a major league record for strikeouts in a nine-inning game on April 29, 1986. How many Seattle Mariners did he fan that day?
        (a) 17
        (b) 18
        (c) 19
        (d) 20

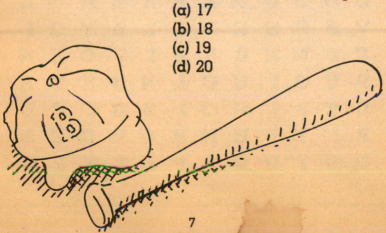

WORD SEARCH

The National League

The National League plays from coast to coast. The 14 NL clubs are listed on the opposite page. Can you find them in the word search? They are hidden horizontally, vertically, backwards, and diagonally.

```
Q M W E G A S T R O S R
S E A S D I F G H J K T
R T L S E V A R B Z X Y
E S E R T Y U N O P L K
G S E T A R I P T K J C
D E X X Z X C M V S N A
O R P P A S S A S D R R
D D O O M E E R N H G D
V A S S E I I L B Y Q I
C P M N B K L I V C X N
P U O I U C L N S Y T A
L K B J H O I S G D F L
P I Y S R R H E W Q E S
Q E T U O P P H F S Z R
```

Atlanta BRAVES

Chicago CUBS

Cincinnati REDS

Colorado ROCKIES

Florida MARLINS

Houston ASTROS

Los Angeles DODGERS

Montreal EXPOS

New York METS

Philadephia PHILLIES

Pittsburgh PIRATES

St. Louis CARDINALS

San Diego PADRES

San Francisco GIANTS

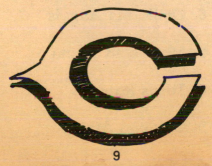

THE MOVING VAN SPECIAL

For decades, baseball teams stayed in their hometowns year after year. But beginning in 1953, the clubs began moving to new locations, usually to attract more fans. See if you can figure out where these modern teams used to be located. Match the answers for Column I and Column II and write them in the blanks on the opposite page.

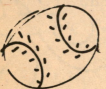

I

1. Los Angeles Dodgers

2. Baltimore Orioles

3. Atlanta Braves

4. Milwaukee Brewers

5. San Francisco Giants

6. California Angels

7. Minnesota Twins

8. Texas Rangers

9. Oakland Athletics

II

A. Kansas City, MO

B. Los Angeles, CA

C. Washington, DC

D. New York, NY

E. Milwaukee, WI

F. Washington, DC (again!)

G. Seattle, WA

H. Brooklyn, NY

I. St. Louis, MO

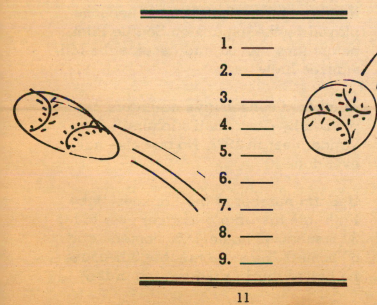

1. ___
2. ___
3. ___
4. ___
5. ___
6. ___
7. ___
8. ___
9. ___

BASEBALL BY THE NUMBERS

Baseball is a game of numbers: numbers of home runs, numbers of victories, numbers on uniforms. Here's a list of numbers and some facts about each one.

0 Uniform number worn by outfielder Oddibe "Call Me O" McDowell, who played for the Texas Rangers.

⅛ Uniform number worn by Eddie Gaedel, a 43" tall midget, who had one plate appearance (he walked) for the 1951 St. Louis Browns.

1 Number of American League seasons played by the expansion Seattle Pilots before they moved and became the Milwaukee Brewers.

2 Number of consecutive no-hitters pitched by Cincinnati's Johnny VanderMeer in 1938. No one else has ever done it.

3 Uniform number of the Yankees' Babe Ruth, the first major-leaguer ever to hit 30 homers, 40 homers, 50 homers, and 60 homers. He wore number 3 because he batted third in the batting order.

4 Babe Ruth set a record by hitting three home runs in a World Series game *twice*. He did it in Game 4 of the 1926 Series and Game 4 of the 1928 Series.

5 The number of consecutive World Series won by the Yankees from 1949 through 1953.

7.11 The combined earned run average of the Pittsburgh Pirates' pitchers in the 1960 World Series. Despite the huge numbers of runs allowed, the Bucs beat the Yankees in seven games, winning the final game on a ninth-inning homer by Bill Mazeroski.

10 The number of home runs hit by slugger Frank Howard during one incredible six-game tear in 1968.

12 The number of one-hitters pitched by Indians' right-hander Bob Feller.

16 The number of unearned runs scored by the New York Mets during a 16–5 victory over the Houston Astros in 1985. The Astros made five errors to let the floodgates open.

22 The number of at bats without a hit by St. Louis shortstop Dal Maxvill during the 1968 World Series.

23 The number of consecutive games lost by the 1961 Philadelphia Phillies.

32 The uniform number worn by National League Most Valuable Player Sandy Koufax and American League MVP Elston Howard in 1963. During the same year, the National Football League MVP was Jim Brown who wore No. 32 for the Cleveland Browns.

56 One of the most famous records in baseball: Joe DiMaggio had at least one hit in 56 straight games in 1941. During the streak, he had 56 singles and scored 56 runs.

60 The number of home runs hit by Babe Ruth in 1927, a record once thought to be unbeatable.

61 The number of home runs hit by the Yankees' Roger Maris in 1961. Because the season had been extended from 154 games to 162 games, baseball people never gave Maris proper credit for his achievement.

96 The uniform number worn by pitcher Bill Voiselle in honor of his hometown, Ninety Six, South Carolina.

120 The number of games lost by the New York Mets in 1962, the team's first season. They won only 40.

COOPERSTOWN QUINTET

Millions of baseball fans visit the Baseball Hall of Fame in Cooperstown, New York. The shrine of the game contains baseball memorabilia along with plaques honoring the sport's all-time greats.

But who were the first to enter the hall? The following five men, each with unique names, were the initial honorees in 1936. Fill in the blanks to learn who they were.

Babe __ __ __ __

Christy __ __ __ __ __ __ __ __ __ __

Ty __ __ __ __

Honus __ __ __ __ __ __

Walter __ __ __ __ __ __ __

BASEBALL SCRAMBLE #1

The answer is JOSE CANSECO. But what is the
question? Unscramble the letters in the words
below to solve this puzzle.

HOW SI HTE OUPRALP UFEDOTIRLE NDA
GLSUREG RDDTAE YB ETH ALNKODA
TLCSAHEIT OT HTE EASTX AGESRNR
LTEA NI ETH 2919 ESNSAO?

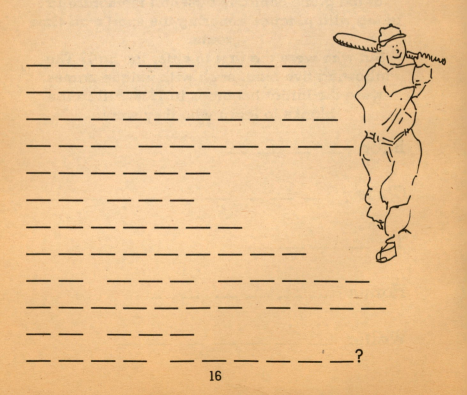

_____ _____ _____ _____ _____

_____ _____ _____

_____ _____ _____ _____ _____

_____ _____ _____ _____ _____

_____ _____ _____ _____

_____ _____ _____ _____ _____

_____ _____ _____ _____ _____

_____ _____ _____ _____ _____ _____

_____ _____ _____ _____ _____ _____

_____ _____ _____

_____ _____ _____ _____ _____ _____ _____ _____?

PICTURE PUZZLE #1

When your team has a runner on third with less than two out, your manager would love his batter to drive in the run. How can he do it? Figure out the picture puzzle and you'll know. Be sure to add or subtract letters as indicated as you go along.

_ _ _ _ _ _ _ _

_ _ _

Answer:

WORD SEARCH

The American League

Do you know the American League? The nicknames of all 14 teams are hidden in the grid below. Can you find them? Some of them are written horizontally, some vertically, some diagonally, and some backwards.

```
M  A  R  I  N  E  R  S  S  O  S  P
A  E  R  N  T  A  A  W  M  G  E  S
X  O  S  D  E  R  E  A  L  Y  L  T
I  M  N  I  P  I  R  Y  T  E  O  R
M  Y  L  A  R  W  O  Q  G  L  I  K
K  A  J  N  H  G  Y  N  F  D  R  S
M  N  N  S  B  V  A  B  R  C  O  C
C  K  X  Z  P  O  L  I  A  U  Y  I
Y  E  T  R  E  U  S  S  N  I  W  T
W  E  Q  L  E  K  J  H  G  H  G  E
F  S  S  J  A  T  I  G  E  R  S  L
Z  X  A  C  V  B  N  M  R  P  O  H
T  Y  B  R  E  W  E  R  S  R  E  T
S  M  X  O  S  E  T  I  H  W  N  A
```

Baltimore ORIOLES

Boston RED SOX

California ANGELS

Chicago WHITE SOX

Cleveland INDIANS

Detroit TIGERS

Kansas City ROYALS

Milwaukee BREWERS

Minnesota TWINS

New York YANKEES

Oakland ATHLETICS

Seattle MARINERS

Texas RANGERS

Toronto BLUE JAYS

YOU'RE THE UMPIRE

Umpires like to say that they have the best seat in baseball — but they have to stand. And sometimes, even on cold days, umpires find themselves in hot water. Umpiring isn't easy — but it helps to know the rules. Do you? Try making the calls in the following situations:

OUT!

1. Tom Glavine is rolling along. His fastball is hopping and his curve is breaking sharply. Against the Dodgers' Darryl Strawberry he bends a curve that barely touches a sliver of the plate as it zips into Greg Olson's mitt. Olson holds the ball in place as Strawberry turns to glare at you. What's the call?

2. The Phillies' Len Dkystra tries to surprise the Mets by bunting for a hit on the first pitch of the game. He drags Doc Gooden's pitch toward first base. A few steps out of the batter's box, he accidentally kicks the ball. Before Met catcher Todd Hundley can pick it up and throw, Dykstra arrives at first base. What's the call?

3. Minnesota's Kent Hrbek lifts a high foul ball toward the Indians' dugout. Cleveland shortstop Mark Lewis races into foul territory and gets a bead on the ball. Near the steps of the dugout, he reaches in and makes the catch — and then tumbles into the dugout. His teammates reach up and keep him from falling. Is this interference?

4. This really happened in 1987: An Atlanta batter lofted a lazy fly ball to left field at Shea Stadium. The Mets' left fielder settled under it, ready to make the catch. Before he could grab it, a flying pigeon swooped in and knocked the ball out of the way, preventing the catch. The batter wound up on second base. What's your call?

5. The Yankees' Don Mattingly lifts a high fly ball deep to right field at Yankee Stadium. Toronto's right fielder Joe Carter goes back, back, back and to the fence. He reaches into the stands, attempting to make the catch. Before he can, a Yankee fan goes for the ball and knocks Carter's arm out of the way. The ball falls into the seats. Carter screams for interference. What's your call?

OH, BROTHER!

There are only around 700 spots on major league rosters every season. It's tough to win a job. But when a family can send two (or more) brothers into the majors, it's quite a feat. Match the all-time brother connections and the all-brother records they hold in Column I with the family names in Column II, and write the letters in the blanks on the opposite page.

I

1. Most strikeouts: Jim and Gaylord

2. Most home runs: Hank and Tommie

3. Most hits: Lloyd and Paul

4. Most runs: Joe, Dom, and Vince

5. Most wins pitched: Phil and Joe

6. Most stolen bases: Honus and Butts

7. Most games: Felipe, Jesus, and Matty

II

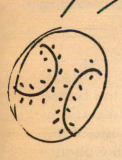

a. Niekro

b. Alou

c. Perry

d. Waner

e. Wagner

f. Aaron

g. DiMaggio

1. ___
2. ___
3. ___
4. ___
5. ___
6. ___
7. ___

COVER QUIZ #2

Tom Glavine

As the Atlanta Braves have gone from the basement to the top of the National League West, left-handed pitcher Tom Glavine has been one of the major driving forces. See what you know about this crafty lefty by circling the correct answers.

1. In addition to the Braves, what other professional sports team also drafted Tom Glavine?

    (a) New England Patriots
    (b) Boston Celtics
    (c) Atlanta Falcons
    (d) Los Angeles Kings

2. When Tom's team won his state high school baseball championship, he pitched nine innings, played the outfield, and knocked in the winning run in extra innings. Tom and his teammates beat Brockton, known best as the hometown of super boxing champ Rocky Marciano. For whom did Tom play?

    (a) Billerica, MA
    (b) Paramus, NJ
    (c) St. Rita, Chicago, IL
    (d) McClymonds, Oakland, CA

3. Glavine has great command of four pitches: fastball, curveball, slider, and one more. This fourth pitch is the one that makes him a consistent winner. What is it?

> (a) a split-fingered fastball
> (b) a spitball
> (c) a two-seam circle change
> (d) a knuckle-curveball

4. Tom won seven games and lost 17 in his first full season with the Braves (1988). Why was his record so terrible?

> (a) The Braves were awful, finishing 54–106. Ugh!
> (b) He would have preferred playing the outfield.
> (c) As a rookie, he had to pitch 10 feet behind the pitching rubber.
> (d) He had a very bad cold.

5. Sometimes Braves' manager Bobby Cox tells the batters who hit *before* Glavine to use a sacrifice bunt. This totally violates baseball tradition. Why does Bobby do it?

> (a) Glavine has promised to share his bonus with him.
> (b) Tom is such a fine batter, he can be trusted to drive runs in.
> (c) Bobby likes to keep the other team guessing.
> (d) Tom pouts in the dugout if he isn't given a chance at some RBIs.

THE NAME GAME

Some ballplayers prefer to use names other than their original first names. We're not even thinking about the Roberts who are called Bob or the Johns known as Jack. Here are some modern examples of real change. Match the names we know in Column I with the players' given first names in Column II, and write the letters in the blanks on the opposite page.

I

1. Bud Black
2. Mike Stanley
3. Nolan Ryan
4. Ben McDonald
5. Gene Harris
6. Craig McMurtry
7. Greg Litton
8. Ricky Jordan
9. Roger Clemens
10. Tony Fernandez
11. Atlee Hammaker
12. Tony Fossas
13. Toby Harrah

14. Cory Snyder
15. Lee Guetterman
16. Andy Hawkins
17. Gene Nelson
18. Rick Dempsey
19. Tim Crews
20. Ken Griffey
21. Dante Bichette
22. Bert Blyleven
23. Lee Stevens
24. Kyle Abbott
25. Tommy Greene

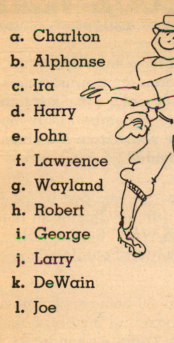

a. Charlton

b. Alphonse

c. Ira

d. Harry

e. John

f. Lawrence

g. Wayland

h. Robert

i. George

j. Larry

k. DeWain

l. Joe

m. Paul

n. Jon

o. Rik

p. Lynn

q. Emilio

r. James

s. Arthur

t. Colbert

u. Stanley

v. William

w. Melton

x. Tyrone

y. Octavio

1. ____
2. ____
3. ____
4. ____
5. ____
6. ____
7. ____
8. ____

9. ____
10. ____
11. ____
12. ____
13. ____
14. ____
15. ____
16. ____

17. ____
18. ____
19. ____
20. ____
21. ____
22. ____
23. ____
24. ____
25. ____

T AT FABULOUS YE R

Baseball has always had its memorable years. Individual player feats, team accomplishments, and unforgettable moments make some seasons, more than others, years to remember. Can you figure out the memorable years from the clues we've provided?

———— **1.** Oakland sweeps the Red Sox in the AL Championship Series; surprising Cincinnati then sweeps the Athletics in the World Series; Nolan Ryan pitches his sixth no-hitter; Pete Rose is banned from baseball.

———— **2.** Babe Ruth swats 60 home runs, one of the most-famous feats in baseball history; Babe's Yankees win the American League pennant by 19 games, then sweep the Pittsburgh Pirates in the World Series.

———— **3.** Cleveland wins 111 games to capture its most-recent American League pennant; the New York Giants then take four straight from the Indians in the World Series, led by a famous catch by Willie Mays and pinch-hitting heroics by Dusty Rhodes.

———— **4.** The Year of the Pitcher. Detroit's Denny McLain wins 31 games. St. Louis' Bob Gibson has an unbelievable 1.12 earned run average and 13 shutouts. Boston's Carl Yastrzemski (.301) is the only American League batter hitting more than .300.

_____ **5.** The New York Mets, who had never finished higher than ninth in the National League, surprise everyone by rolling to victory in the new NL East. Then they sweep Atlanta in the play-offs and overcome heavily favored Baltimore, 4 games to 1, in the World Series.

_____ **6.** New York Giants' left-hander Carl Hubbell strikes out future Hall of Famers Babe Ruth, Lou Gehrig, Jimmie Foxx, Al Simmons, and Joe Cronin in order during the second All-Star Game ever. Nonetheless, the American League wins, 9–7.

_____ **7.** The Atlanta Braves, dead last in the NL the previous year, zoom to the top of the NL West, then defeat the Pittsburgh Pirates in the NL Championship Series. Only a perfect performance at home allows the Minnesota Twins to defeat the Braves in the World Series.

_____ **8.** Joe DiMaggio of the Yankees hits safely in 56 straight games; Ted Williams of Boston bats .406, the last major-leaguer to hit .400 or better; the Brooklyn Dodgers win their first pennant in 21 years but lose to DiMaggio's Yankees in the World Series.

_____ **9.** The American League expands from eight teams to 10; the Yankees' Roger Maris hits 61 home runs to break Babe Ruth's all-time mark, but the season is now eight games longer; Mickey Mantle hits 54 homers but loses the title to his teammate Maris.

PICTURE PUZZLE #2

Since 1933, the best players in the American and National Leagues gather to entertain all baseball fans. (In fact, some years they got together twice!) What is this contest called? Figure out the picture puzzle and you'll know. Be sure to add or subtract letters as indicated as you go along.

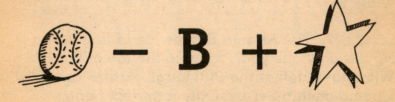

_ _ _ _ - _ _ _ _

 — RPES + ME

_ _ _ _

Answer:

BASEBALL SCRAMBLE #2

The answer is DEION SANDERS. But what is the question? Unscramble the letters in the words below to solve this puzzle.

HWO SI TEH ALEYRP OHW IHST NAD
ILDFES OFR ETH TATLNAA RVSBAE
UIGDRN ETH UMESMR NAD KOSKCN
DWNO PSSSEA ADN RTRNEUS IKCSK ROF
ETH TATLNAA ACNSFLO VREEY ALFL?

_____ __ ___ _____ ___ ____ ___
_____ ___ ___ _____ _____
_____ ___ _____ ___ _____
____ _____ ___ _____ _____ ___
___ _____ _____ _____ ____?

1947 OR BUST?

When World Series history students get together, it doesn't take them long to turn to memories of the 1947 Series. The Brooklyn Dodgers and New York Yankees were the contenders, marking the first of six times they would meet over the next 10 years. Jackie Robinson, who had become the first black man ever to play in the major leagues that spring, became the first to play in a World Series that fall.

Some of the most memorable moments come from games four and six. In game four at Brooklyn's Ebbets Field, Yankee right-hander Bill Bevens held the Dodgers without a hit until the ninth inning. No one had ever pitched a World Series no-hitter. Brooklyn scored a run on a bases-loaded walk in the fifth inning. But the Dodgers trailed, 2–1, starting the bottom of the ninth.

Bevens got two men out but walked two others, his ninth and tenth walks of the game. Then, pinch-hitter Cookie Lavagetto stepped up to the plate. He smashed a double off the wall in right field and both runners scored. Bevens lost his no-hitter and the game with one swing of Cookie's bat.

Two days later, back at Yankee Stadium, New York had taken a 5–4 lead in the fifth inning and threatened to blow the game open. Joe DiMaggio smacked a long fly to the bullpen in left, but Dodger outfielder Al Gionfriddo raced back to the fence and robbed DiMag. It was one of the most famous World Series catches ever. The Dodgers went on to win, 8–6.

For Bevens, Lavagetto, and Gionfriddo, these were special moments. But another "weird moment" links them forever in baseball history. What was it?

THE CY YOUNG CROSSWORD

Since 1956, the Baseball Writers Association of America has presented the Cy Young Award to the best pitcher in the game. From 1956 to 1966, it went to only one pitcher in the major leagues. Since 1967, one pitcher in each league has taken the trophy. It is named for the winningest pitcher (511 victories) in the history of baseball. Can you complete the Cy Young Crossword with the clues we've provided on the opposite page?

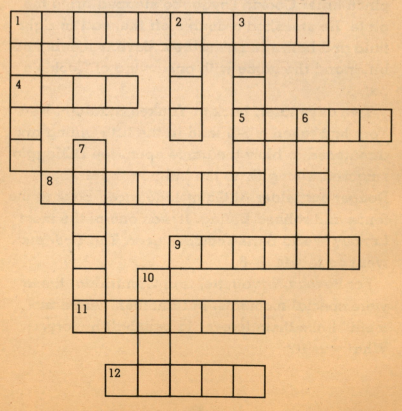

Across

1. AL winner for Kansas City in '85 and '89, now with the New York Mets: Bret _____.

4. First name of 1988 Dodger hero: _____ Hershiser.

5. Star of Padre staff in 1989: Mark _____.

8. The Phillies' ace who won in '72 and '80: lefty Steve _____.

9. One of the greatest lefties ever and winner in '63, '65, and '66: Dodgers' Hall of Famer Sandy _____.

11. First name of A's reliever and '81 winner: _____ Fingers.

12. A winner in both leagues, in '72 with Cleveland and in '78 with San Diego: Gaylord _____.

Down

1. Star of the Houston staff in '86: righty Mike _____.

2. Chubby White Sox ace and '83 winner: Lamarr _____.

3. Called Doctor, Mets' 1985 winner: Dwight _____.

6. He makes sweet music as he did in winning for the Twins in '88: lefty Frank _____.

7. Known for underwear commercials these days, this Oriole won three times ('73, '75, '76): Jim _____.

10. Leader of the Athletics' pitchers in '71, he was true and Vida _____.

T ERE ONCE WAS
BALLPARK HERE

Until the Baltimore Orioles built their new Camden Yards ballpark, most big league teams were moving into new stadiums that lacked the charm of the old fields. See if you can match up the classic stadiums in Column I with the teams that played there in Column II, and write the letters in the blanks on the opposite page.

I

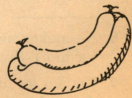

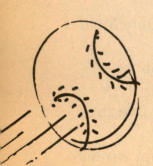

1. Ebbets Field

2. Seals Stadium

3. Forbes Field

4. Polo Grounds

5. Crosley Field

6. Sportsman's Park

7. Jarry Park

8. The Coliseum

9. Memorial Stadium

10. Connie Mack Stadium

II

a. New York Giants

b. St. Louis Cardinals

c. Baltimore Orioles

d. Philadelphia Phillies

e. Brooklyn Dodgers

f. Los Angeles Dodgers

g. Cincinnati Reds

h. San Francisco Giants

i. Montreal Expos

j. Pittsburgh Pirates

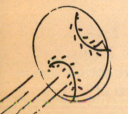

1. ____   6. ____

2. ____   7. ____

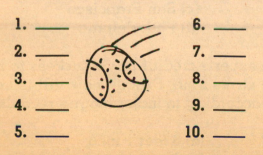

3. ____   8. ____

4. ____   9. ____

5. ____   10. ____

COVER QUIZ #3

Kirby Puckett

He's built more like a bowling ball than a baseball player. But when it looked like Kirby Puckett could become a free agent after the 1992 season, the entire state of Minnesota protested mightily. Kirby hits, hits with power, runs, fields, and throws — which is just about it in baseball. See how much you know about this center fielder by circling the correct answers.

1. When Kirby's contract talks with the Twins broke down in '92, there were rumors that he might head back to his hometown of _____.

   (a) Chicago
   (b) Sheboygan
   (c) San Francisco
   (d) Philadelphia

2. Some experts credit Kirby's success to his small strike zone. Exactly how tall is he, at least according to major league records?

   (a) 6 feet 1 inch
   (b) 4 feet 11 inches
   (c) 5 feet 8 inches
   (d) 5 feet 4 inches

3. Puckett led the Twins to two world championships through the end of the '92 season. Minnesota won both Series by winning all four home games. What were those fabulous years?

      (a) 1986 and 1990
      (b) 1988 and 1990
      (c) 1984 and 1988
      (d) 1987 and 1991

4. Despite enjoying a great '91 season, Kirby finished in the top ten American-Leaguers in only two major categories. They were:

   (a) runs scored and home runs
   (b) batting and hits
   (c) stolen bases and on-base percentage
   (d) hot-dog eating and autograph signing

5. When Kirby smacked 234 hits in 1988, he came within five hits of tying the all-time Twins' record in that category. Who's the Hall of Fame record holder in Twin hits?

      (a) Rod Carew
      (b) Kent Hrbek
      (c) Zoilo Versalles
      (d) Harmon Killebrew

6. How did Puckett become a Twin? (Obviously, someone in the Minnesota front office knew what he was doing.)

   (a) free agent in 1985
   (b) traded to Minnesota by Baltimore in 1984
   (c) first-round draft pick in 1982
   (d) showed up one day and demanded a tryout

MVP CROSSWORD

Every season since 1931, baseball writers have selected the Most Valuable Player in each league. Each winner has enjoyed a super season and, usually, his team has won a title. See if you can complete the crossword from the clues given on the opposite page.

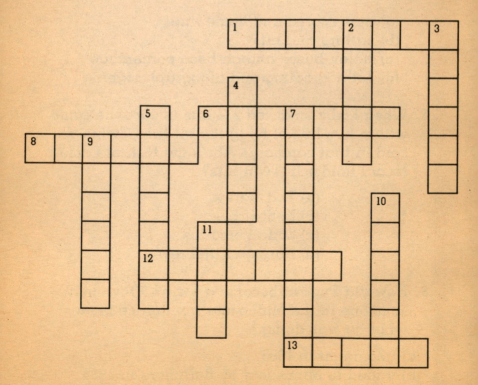

Across

1. NL 1984 winner: Chicago second-baseman Ryne _____.

6. Three-time NL winner ('80, '81, '86): Phillie third-sacker Mike _____.

8. NL winner in '75 and '76, now an ESPN broadcaster: Cincinnati second-baseman Little Joe _____.

12. AL 1986 winner, still starring for Boston; pitcher Roger _____.

13. AL 1989 winner, who got his 3,000th hit in 1992: Milwaukee outfielder Robin _____.

Down

2. NL 1990 leader as a Pirate outfielder: Barry _____.

3. NL 1988 winner hit a memorable World Series homer: then-Dodger outfielder Kirk _____.

4. Led the Cardinals in 1985, now a Giant outfielder: Willie _____.

5. Oakland slugger won it in 1988, now with Texas: outfielder Jose _____.

7. 1985 AL winner: Yankee first-sacker Don _____ does it all.

9. 1983 AL victor never misses a game: Baltimore shortstop Cal _____.

10. The Hawk won in '87 for the Cubs: outfielder Andre _____.

11. Now toiling for Chicago, 1987 winner was Toronto outfielder George _____.

BASEBALL MATH

You think you know baseball? You're sure you know math? If you do, you'll have no trouble solving the Super Baseball Trivia Question on the opposite page.

1. The number of players on the regular major league roster. ____

2. The number of games played by each team each season. ____

3. The number of home runs hit by Babe Ruth in 1927. ____

4. The number of World Series won by the Chicago Cubs since 1908. ____

5. The number of times Philadelphia's Mike Schmidt led the National League in home runs. ____

Now, add the numbers above and write your answer in this box. ☐

Subtract Jackie Robinson's uniform number (42) and write the answer in this box. ☐

Finally, multiply by 10.

Now, you have the answer to the Super Baseball Trivia Question on the opposite page.

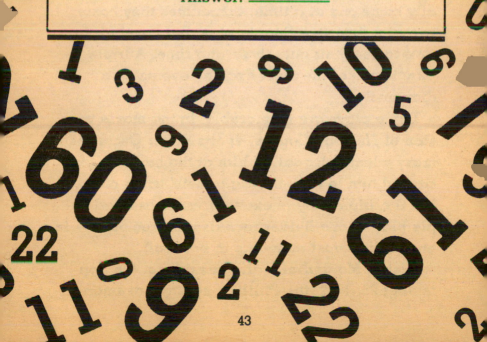

SUPER BASEBALL TRIVIA QUESTION

How many consecutive games did the New York Yankees' Lou Gehrig play in between 1925 and 1939?

Answer: _____

THREE 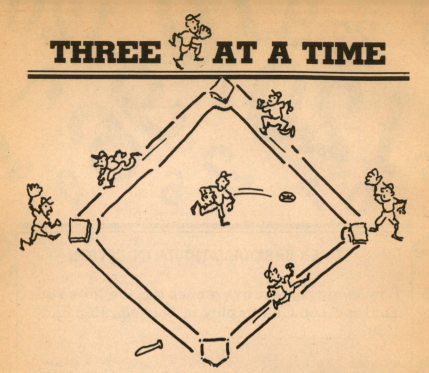 AT A TIME

Each team gets 27 outs in a game. They usually come one at a time. Sometimes they come two at a time — a double play. But baseball fans love to see their outs three at a time. A triple play is one of the most exciting events on a diamond.

Triple plays are memorable. In the movie version of *The Odd Couple*, sports writer Oscar went crazy when Felix called him at the ballpark and caused him to miss seeing a Mets' triple play. But if a triple play is exciting; an *unassisted* triple play — one fielder records all three outs — is one of the rarest moments in baseball.

Mickey Morandini is the latest hero. On September 20, 1992, the Phillies' second baseman became only the ninth major-leaguer ever to ring up an unassisted triple play. The rival Pirates had Andy Van Slyke on second and Barry Bonds on first in the bottom of the sixth inning. With the runners going on the pitch, Pittsburgh's Jeff King lined a shot toward center field. Morandini dived to his right, snagged the ball to get King out, stepped on second to retire Van Slyke, and tagged Bonds who had reached second base. It was the majors' first unassisted triple play since July 30, 1968, when the Washington Senators' Ron Hansen had pulled it off.

The most famous unassisted triple play ever? It was the only one in World Series history. Cleveland second-baseman Bill Wambsganss snared a line drive off the bat of Brooklyn pitcher Clarence Mitchell to start his one-man, three-out play. The year was 1920.

Now for the unassisted triple play Super Trivia question: Before Morandini's feat, the last National League unassisted triple play had occurred on May 30, 1927. That's when Chicago Cub Jimmy Cooney retired three Pittsburgh Pirates on one swing of Paul Waner's bat. The question: How much longer did it take before the major leagues' *next* unassisted triple play?

(a) one day
(b) ten years
(c) 14 years
(d) 21 years

It's one of the most exciting plays in baseball. There isn't a more productive hit. Bases loaded and a slugger at the plate; here comes the pitch, and there it goes. Figure out the picture puzzle and you'll know what this power play is called. Be sure to add or subtract letters as indicated as you go along.

GR + &

 – IDE + AM

_ _ _ _ _ _ _ - _

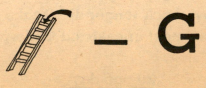 – G

_ _ _ _

Answer:

NUMBER TRIVIA

Billy Herman's family prepared their household budget differently from any other family. During a sparkling career (he hit .304 for 13 years), he played in four World Series — one every three years. Billy collected Series shares with the 1932, 1935, and 1938 Cubs and the 1941 Dodgers.

One must have been Reggie Jackson's lucky number. In Game 6 of the 1977 World Series, Reggie took one swing in each of three at bats. The result: three home runs.

One wasn't exactly as lucky for pitcher Hoyt Wilhelm. He homered in his first major-league at bat, for the New York Giants in 1952. He went on to play 21 seasons in the majors. He never hit another homer.

Here's another one-day wonder. Mike Parrott of the Seattle Mariners was the winning pitcher on opening day in 1980. He should have packed it in right there. His final season record was 1–16.

On the flip side, second-baseman Joe Gordon played seven of his 11 major-league seasons with the New York Yankees. During those seven campaigns, he played exactly 1,000 games. How many hits did he have? Exactly 1,000!

ANSWERS

Page 4
Starting Lineup

1. F
2. H
3. B
4. J
5. A
6. I
7. E
8. D
9. G
10. C

Page 6
Cover Quiz #1
Roger Clemens

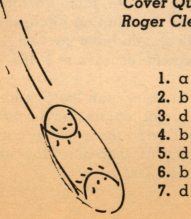

1. a
2. b
3. d
4. b
5. d
6. b
7. d

Word Search
The National League

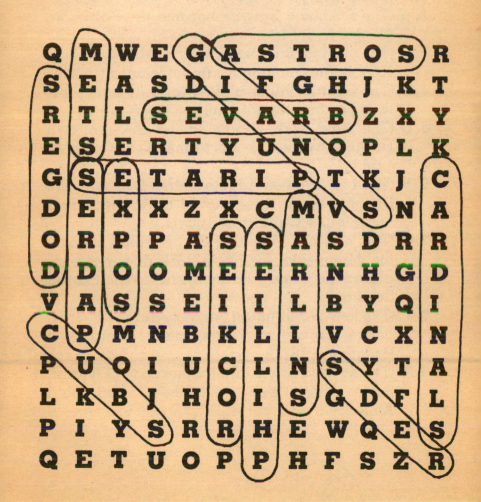

Q M W E G A S T R O S R
S E A S D I F G H J K T
R T L S E V A R B Z X Y
E S E R T Y U N O P L K
G S E T A R I P T K J C
D E X X Z X C M V S N A
O R P P A S S A S D R R
D D O O M E E R N H G D
V A S S E I I L B Y Q I
C P M N B K L I V C X N
P U Q I U C L N S Y T A
L K B J H O I S G D F L
P I Y S R R H E W Q E S
Q E T U O P P H F S Z R

1. **H** (The Brooklyn Dodgers moved west in 1958.)
2. **I** (The St. Louis Browns became the Baltimore Orioles in 1954.)
3. **E** (The Boston Braves moved to Milwaukee in 1953, before moving again to Atlanta.)
4. **G** (The Seattle Pilots played for only one year, then became the Milwaukee Brewers.)
5. **D** (The New York Giants joined the Brooklyn Dodgers in their move to the West Coast in 1958.)
6. **B** (The Los Angeles Angels shared L.A. with the Dodgers before they moved to Anaheim and became the California Angels.)
7. **C** (The original Washington Senators became the Minnesota Twins in 1961 and were replaced the same year by the new Washington Senators.)
8. **F** (The new Washington Senators didn't last long before moving to Texas and becoming the Rangers in 1972.)
9. **A** (The Kansas City Athletics moved to Oakland. Before that, they were the Philadelphia Athletics.)

Page 15
Cooperstown
Quintet

B a b e R U T H

Christy M A T H E W S O N

T y C O B B

H o n u s W A G N E R

W a l t e r J O H N S O N

Page 16
Baseball Scramble
#1

WHO IS THE POPULAR OUTFIELDER AND
SLUGGER TRADED BY THE OAKLAND
ATHLETICS TO THE TEXAS RANGERS LATE
IN THE 1992 SEASON?

Page 17
Picture Puzzle #1

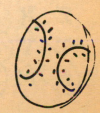

SACRIFICE FLY

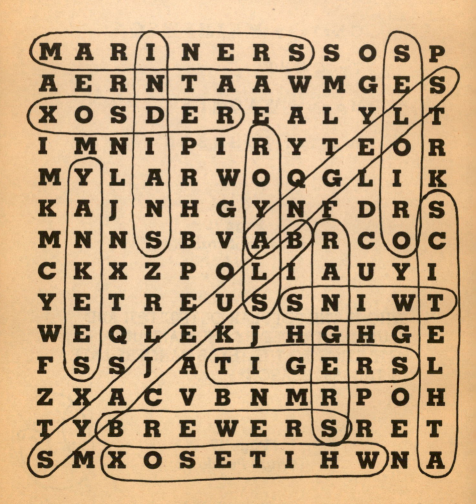

1. If any part of the ball touches any part of the strike zone, it's a strike. That's why Glavine is so good.

2. Lenny is out. He made contact with the ball in fair territory, an automatic out. If he had kicked the ball while in foul territory or if he was still in the batter's box, it would just have been a strike.

3. This is not interference, and Hrbek is out. It's perfectly legal for players in the dugout to keep a player on the field from falling. Chances are, if Lewis was falling into the Twins' dugout, no one would have helped him.

4. It's a two-base hit. If a thrown or batted ball hits any flying object, the ball remains in play.

5. It's a home run. The players own the playing field. The fans own the stands. Once Carter "joined" the spectators, he was at his own risk.

Page 22
Oh, Brother!

1. c
2. f
3. d
4. g
5. a
6. e
7. b

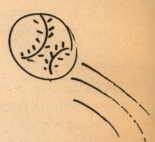

Page 24
Cover Quiz #2
Tom Glavine

1. d (The National Hockey League Kings took potential-star Glavine in the fourth round!)
2. a
3. c
4. a
5. b

1. d
2. h
3. p
4. j
5. x
6. l
7. n
8. m
9. v
10. y
11. a
12. q
13. t
14. r
15. s
16. w
17. g
18. e
19. u
20. i
21. b
22. o
23. k
24. f
25. c

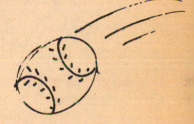

Page 28
That Fabulous Year

1. 1990
2. 1927
3. 1954
4. 1968
5. 1969
6. 1934
7. 1991
8. 1941
9. 1961

Page 30
Picture Puzzle #2

ALL-STAR GAME

WHO IS THE PLAYER WHO HITS AND FIELDS
FOR THE ATLANTA BRAVES DURING THE
SUMMER AND KNOCKS DOWN PASSES AND
RETURNS KICKS FOR THE ATLANTA FALCONS
EVERY FALL?

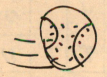

Page 32
1947 or Bust?

After the 1947 World Series, none of the three ever
played in a major league game again!

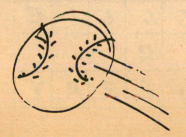

Page 34
The Cy Young Crossword

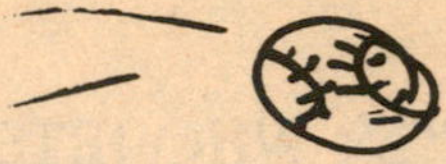

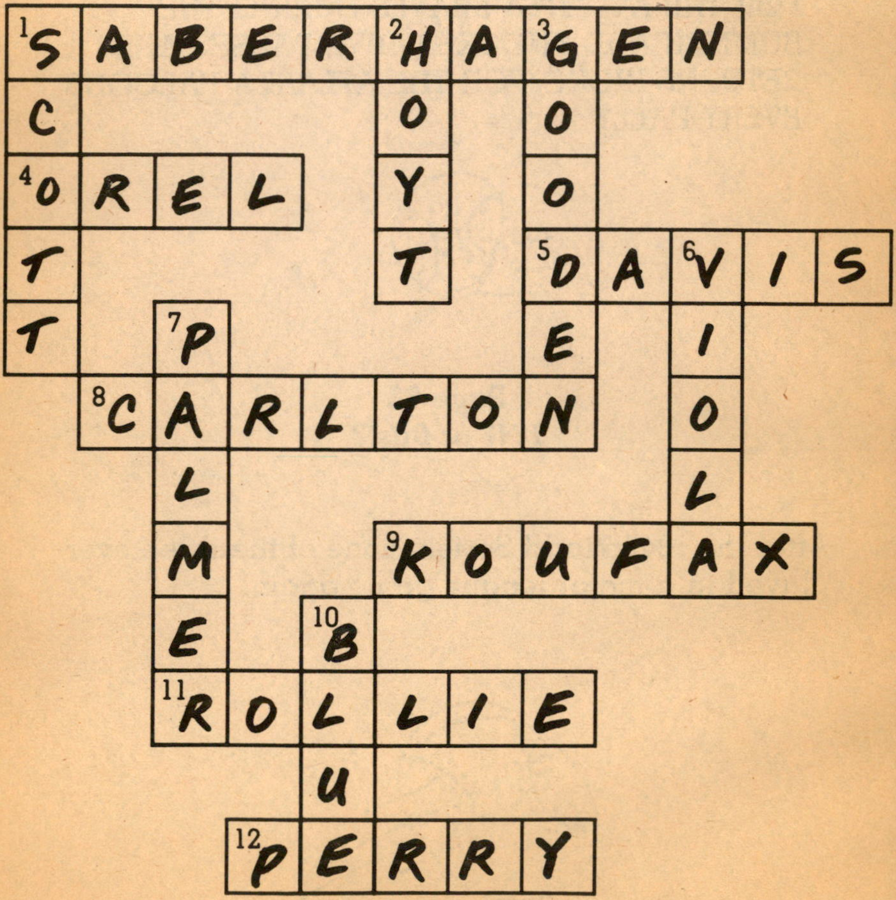

1 SABERHAGEN
2 HOYT
3 GOODEN
4 OREL
1 SCOTT
5 DAVIS
6 VIOLA
7 PALMER
8 CARLTON
9 KOUFAX
10 BLUE
11 ROLLIE
12 PERRY

Page 36
There Once Was a
Ballpark Here

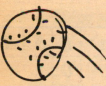

1. e
2. h
3. j
4. a
5. g
6. b
7. i
8. f
9. c
10. d

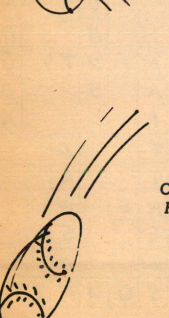

Page 38
Cover Quiz #3
Kirby Puckett

1. a
2. c
3. d
4. b
5. a
6. c

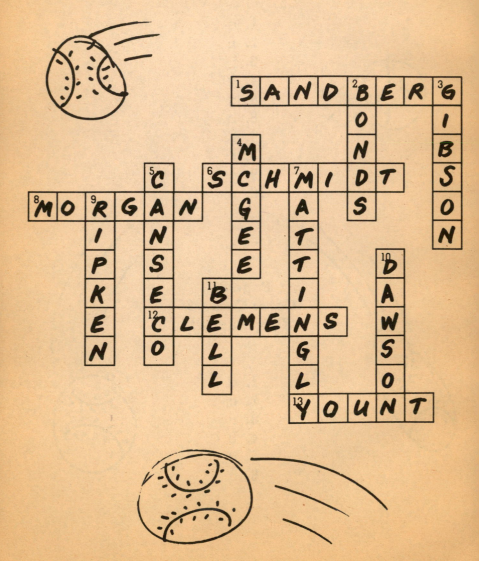

$$25 + 162 + 60 + 0 \text{ (surprise!)} + 8 = 255$$

$$255 - 42 = 213$$

$$213 \times 10 = 2{,}130$$

Page 44
Three at a Time

(a) One day. On May 31, 1927, first-baseman Johnny Neun of the American League's Detroit Tigers caught a liner off the bat of Cleveland's Homer Summa. He tagged out Charlie Jamieson, then ran to second to retire slow-footed Glen Myatt. After two unassisted triple plays on consecutive days, there wasn't another until Hansen got his 41 years and two months later!

GRAND-SLAM HOME RUN

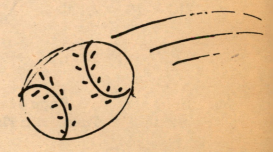

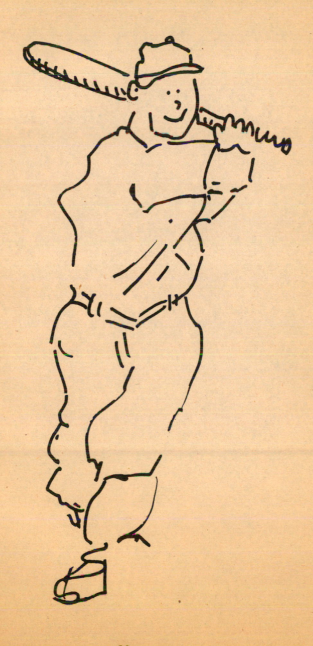